Success is my duty to society.

Why is this meaningful to me?

How did I use this motivation today to move toward my purpose?

Success is my duty to myself.

Why is this meaningful to me?

How did I use this motivation today to move toward my purpose?

Success is my duty to my immediate family.

Why is this meaningful to me?

How did I use this motivation today to move toward my purpose?

Success is my duty to my future lineage & legacy.

Why is this meaningful to me?

How did I use this motivation today to move toward my purpose?

In direct sales either I make money, or I build character.

Why is this meaningful to me?

How did I use this motivation today to move toward my purpose?

Every day is a new opportunity to learn.

Why is this meaningful to me?

How did I use this motivation today to move toward my purpose?

Every day is an opportunity to find ppl to grow and mentor as I grow.

Why is this meaningful to me?

How did I use this motivation today to move toward my purpose?

Produce income. I need it to survive.

Why is this meaningful to me?

How did I use this motivation today to move toward my purpose?

I will improve my skill and learn from my mistakes.

Why is this meaningful to me?

How did I use this motivation today to move toward my purpose?

I am helping people with my product or service.

Why is this meaningful to me?

How did I use this motivation today to move toward my purpose?

Develop "tough skin". This skill will set me up for unlimited success.

Why is this meaningful to me?

How did I use this motivation today to move toward my purpose?

I meet great quality people and leave a positive lasting impression.

Why is this meaningful to me?

How did I use this motivation today to move toward my purpose?

Every interaction is a chance to enhance my skills.

Why is this meaningful to me?

How did I use this motivation today to move toward my purpose?

Be a leader by building teams & helping the people around me.

Why is this meaningful to me?

How did I use this motivation today to move toward my purpose?

Perfect my pitch with different word tracks/tones.

Why is this meaningful to me?

How did I use this motivation today to move toward my purpose?

Somebody out there is working hard to beat me (and working harder than me).

Why is this meaningful to me?

How did I use this motivation today to move toward my purpose?

Good things come to those who hustle.

Why is this meaningful to me?

How did I use this motivation today to move toward my purpose?

I can get food after this (or frozen yogurt).

Why is this meaningful to me?

How did I use this motivation today to move toward my purpose?

Make lasting impression on my superiors. This results in more opportunity.

Why is this meaningful to me?

How did I use this motivation today to move toward my purpose?

Create income so I can invest and multiply.

Why is this meaningful to me?

How did I use this motivation today to move toward my purpose?

I will make a positive impact with unique talents & opportunities I've been given.

Why is this meaningful to me?

How did I use this motivation today to move toward my purpose?

My achievement will never grow above my ability to grow & help others.

Why is this meaningful to me?

How did I use this motivation today to move toward my purpose?

I feel happy with life when I push my potential.

Why is this meaningful to me?

How did I use this motivation today to move toward my purpose?

I will make my family proud.

Why is this meaningful to me?

How did I use this motivation today to move toward my purpose?

With great adversity comes great prosperity.

Why is this meaningful to me?

How did I use this motivation today to move toward my purpose?

I owe it to my future self.

Why is this meaningful to me?

How did I use this motivation today to move toward my purpose?

I owe it to my company.

Why is this meaningful to me?

How did I use this motivation today to move toward my purpose?

I owe it to my (future) kids.

Why is this meaningful to me?

How did I use this motivation today to move toward my purpose?

I owe it to my spouse or significant other.

Why is this meaningful to me?

How did I use this motivation today to move toward my purpose?

I have the same amount of hours in a day as the richest man in the world.

Why is this meaningful to me?

How did I use this motivation today to move toward my purpose?

I have the same # of hours in a day as the smartest man in the world.

Why is this meaningful to me?

How did I use this motivation today to move toward my purpose?

I will sacrifice my time now to achieve time freedom in the future.

Why is this meaningful to me?

How did I use this motivation today to move toward my purpose?

The only time success comes before work is in the dictionary.

Why is this meaningful to me?

How did I use this motivation today to move toward my purpose?

You never know who you may connect with.

Why is this meaningful to me?

How did I use this motivation today to move toward my purpose?

If I did it before I can do it again.

Why is this meaningful to me?

How did I use this motivation today to move toward my purpose?

Today I will *MASTER* my confidence.

Why is this meaningful to me?

How did I use this motivation today to move toward my purpose?

I will learn how to properly communicate with body language.

Why is this meaningful to me?

How did I use this motivation today to move toward my purpose?

I will keep a positive attitude through adversity.

Why is this meaningful to me?

How did I use this motivation today to move toward my purpose?

FAILURE IS IMPOSSIBLE!!! **The only way I can fail is by accepting failure and quitting. So decide not to quit and commit.**

Why is this meaningful to me?

How did I use this motivation today to move toward my purpose?

The more I finish each day the more motivated I become.

Why is this meaningful to me?

How did I use this motivation today to move toward my purpose?

The harder I challenge myself the more *confident* I will become.

Why is this meaningful to me?

How did I use this motivation today to move toward my purpose?

In any given moment of adversity, we have two choices. Back down or push forward. The choice is mine.

Why is this meaningful to me?

How did I use this motivation today to move toward my purpose?